Counting 1 to 10

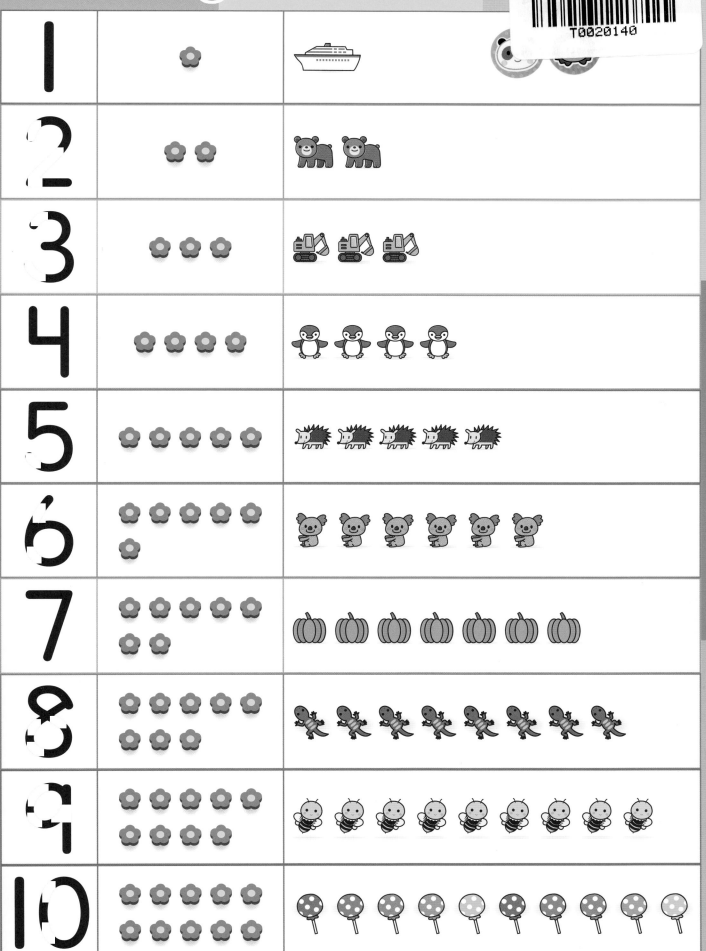

Counting 11 to 20 → Page 60

Trace the Number 1

To Parents: Encourage your child to trace with a crayon. If they have difficulty using the crayon independently, have them trace with a finger first. Then, guide your children's hand to help them trace the number. After tracing is done, say "one flower" and "one unicorn."

  Trace the number 1 and say "one flower" and "one unicorn."

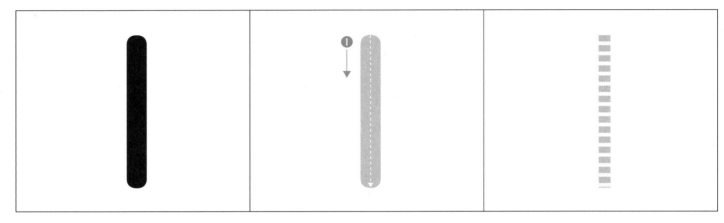

ONE

  Find 1 ship and circle it. Then, find the number 1.

example

Color the Unicorn

Good job!

   Trace the number 1 from ➡ to ➡. Then, color the unicorn and add a golden horn sticker.

Trace the Number 2

To Parents: The numbers and arrows noted on each number diagram indicate the proper form used when writing. Encourage your child to trace with a crayon. If they have difficulty using the crayon independently, have them trace with a finger first.

  Trace the number 2 and say "two flowers" and "two monsters."

TWO

  Find 2 bears and circle them. Then, find the number 2.

Add Stickers and Fold

To Parents: Ask your child questions to spark curiosity! Ask how many eyes, teeth, hands, and feet the monster has. If your child is having difficulty folding the page, fold it for them.

 First add the antenna and eye stickers. Then, fold along the dotted lines for a surprise!

Trace the Number 3

To Parents: Ask your child to say the number aloud as they trace it with a crayon. If they have difficulty using the crayon independently, have them trace with a finger first. Then, ask to count the flowers and police cars out loud. Explain that the objects are different but there are three of each.

  Trace the number 3 and say "three flowers" and "three police cars."

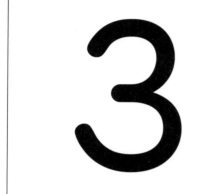

THREE

  Find 3 excavators and circle them. Then, find the number 3.

Count the Vehicles

To Parents: Encourage your child to press their finger on each vehicle and count aloud. Once the groups of three have been circled, ask your child how many circles there are. It's fine if your child circled different vehicles as long as it's a group of three.

 Circle each group of 3 vehicles. How many groups of 3 are there?

example

Trace the Number 4

To Parents: When tracing the number 4, your child will need to make two lines, picking up the crayon in between. Trace the 4 with your finger to demonstrate as you explain this to your child.

  Trace the number 4 and say "four flowers" and "four pigs."

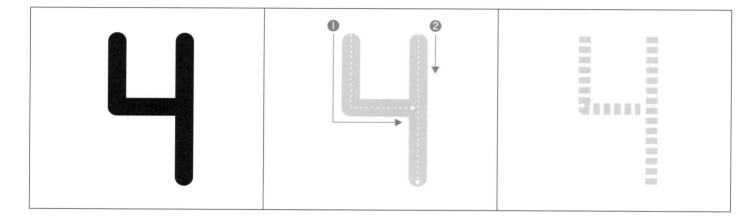

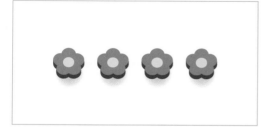 

FOUR

  Find 4 penguins and circle them. Then, find the number 4.

Count the Pigs

To Parents: When you provide your child with the pig stickers, ask them to count them. Then, count aloud together as your child places the stickers on the path. Encourage your child to count other animals on the page too!

Place the pig stickers on the path. Then, trace the path with your finger from  to ➡.

10

Trace the Number 5

To Parents: The number 5 requires drawing two separate lines. Demonstrate how to draw with your finger first. Then, encourage your child to try.

 Trace the number 5 and say "five flowers" and "five chicks."

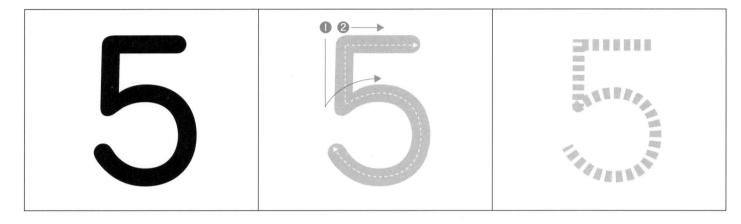

FIVE

Find 5 hedgehogs and circle them. Then, find the number 5.

Count the Chicks

To Parents: This activity helps your child build recognition skills. Help them by asking about each animal's color and other details. Then, ask your child to point to and count each chick. After they have circled the chicks, encourage them to say "five chicks, one squirrel, and one mouse."

 Circle five chicks.

example

Trace the Number 6

To Parents: The number 6 is written as one continuous, curved line that loops back on itself. Demonstrate how to draw with your finger first. Then, encourage your child to try.

  Trace the number 6 and say "six flowers" and "six hats."

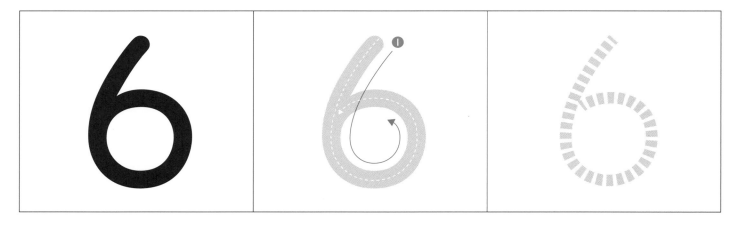

SIX

 Find 6 koalas and circle them. Then, find the number 6.

Count the Hats

To Parents: First, ask your child to point to, press on, and count the children in the picture. Then ask, "If each child gets one hat, how many hats do we need?"

 Count the children aloud. Then, put a hat sticker on each child.

Trace the Number 7

To Parents: Have your child focus on tracing the number 7. Then, draw their attention to the groups of flowers and apples. Encourage them to press a finger on each object when counting.

 Trace the number 7 and say "seven flowers" and "seven apples."

 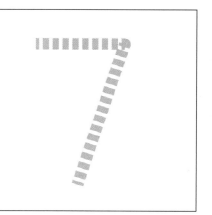

SEVEN

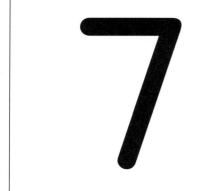 Find 7 pumpkins and circle them. Then, find the number 7.

Count the Apples

To Parents: Provide your child with a red crayon. After they have colored three apples, ask them how many more apples they will color and count the remaining apples. Then, count the colored apples aloud together.

Sticker

Good job!

 Color the apples and count them.

Sticker
Good job!

Trace the Number 8

To Parents: When a child counts several objects, they may lose track. Your child can color, circle, or draw a line through the objects in order to visually recognize what has and hasn't been counted.

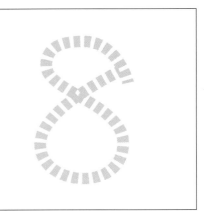

  Trace the number 8 and say "eight flowers" and "eight leaves."

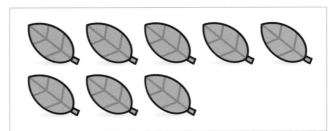

EIGHT

 Find 8 lizards and circle them. Then, find the number 8.

Count the Leaves

To Parents: Start by asking, "How many eyes does a face have?" Then, let your child choose stickers for the eyes. Do this with each part of the face until all the stickers have been placed. Count them together. When done, praise your child by saying "It looks great!"

  Place the 8 leaf stickers on the circle to make a face. Draw to add hair.

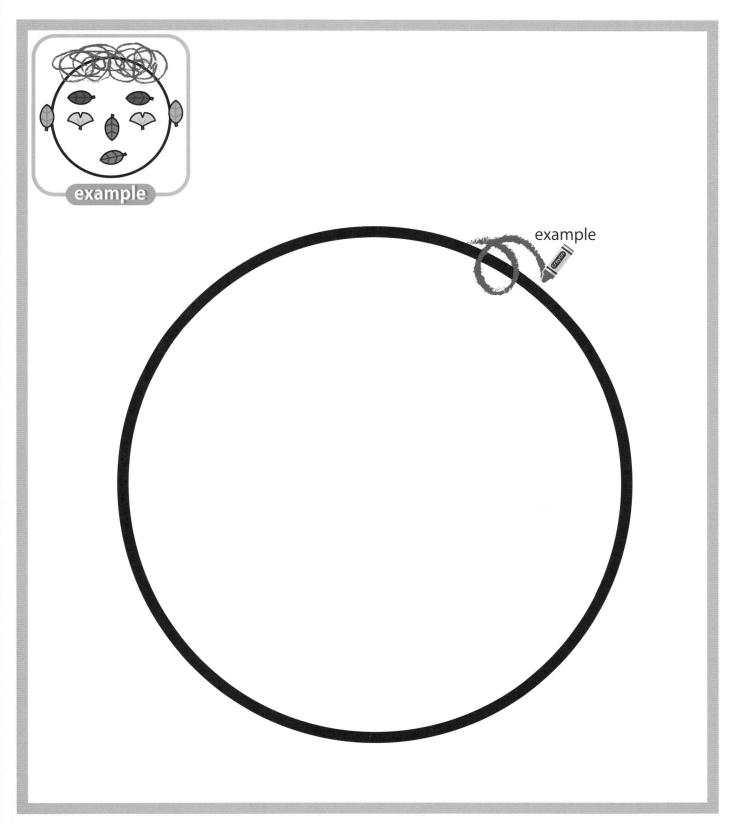

example

example

Trace the Number 9

To Parents: Have your child trace the number 9. Then, encourage them to count the flowers and ants.

 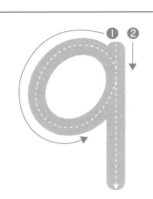 Trace the number 9 and say "nine flowers" and "nine ants."

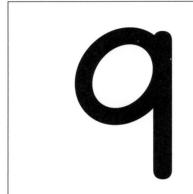 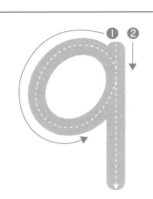 

NINE

  Find 9 bees and circle them. Then, find the number 9.

Count the Ants

To Parents: Have your child trace the ants' path with a finger and count them aloud. Let your child say "nine" each time they fold the page and "ants" each time they unfold it.

 Trace a line from ➡ to ➡. Count the ants as you go. Then, fold the page for a surprise!

Fold up

Fold down

20

Trace the Number 10

To Parents: Each time your child counts a flower or ghost, make sure they point to it with their finger. Try placing ten objects on the table and count them together.

  Trace a number 10 and say "ten flowers" and "ten ghosts."

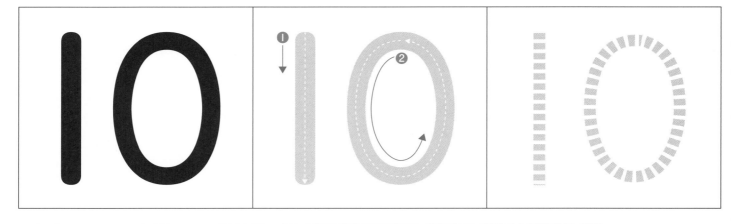

TEN

  Find 10 lollipops and circle them. Then, find the number 10.

Count the Ghosts

To Parents: Cut out and put glue on the ghosts for your child. Then, let them place the ghosts on the boxes labeled "paste." Count all the ghosts together!

 Paste the ghosts onto the yellow boxes. Count the ghosts aloud. What do you see?

Parents: Cut out the ghosts for your child. Then, add glue.

Compare the Quantities

To Parents: Encourage your child to count the puppies. Then, ask them how many dog bowls you'll need to feed the puppies. If this is difficult for your child, count the empty bowls together. This activity teaches one-to-one correspondence.

 Feed the puppies by placing the dog bowl stickers in front of them.

glue	glue	glue	glue

Compare the Quantities

To Parents: Drawing lines will help your child see if there are the same number of balloons as there are children. Explain this to your child using the example provided. Then, ask them to give each child one balloon by drawing three more strings.

  Are there more balloons or children in this picture? Connect each balloon string to each child's hand to find out. Then, fold the page to confirm.

example

Fold up

How to Play

Parents: Cut along the gray line for your child.

Compare the Quantities

To Parents: Let your child peel off each sticker from the sticker sheet to help build fine motor skills. Encourage them to count the monkeys and bananas separately to be sure that there are the same number of each.

 Give each monkey a banana sticker.

There is 1 extra balloon!

Compare the Quantities

To Parents: Point to the example and say "Let's give one fish to each cat." Then, ask your child to draw a line from each cat to each fish until they run out of fish. Are there enough fish? Ask your child.

Are there more cats than fish in the picture? Draw lines to find out. Then, fold the page to confirm.

How to Play

Fold up

example

Sticker
Good job!

Which has More?

To Parents: Let your child practice judging "less or more" visually without counting the fries. Ask which plate looks like it has more on it. One clue you can give is that the bigger portion covers up more of the plate!

 Which plate has more fries? Color the ◯ below the bigger serving of fries.

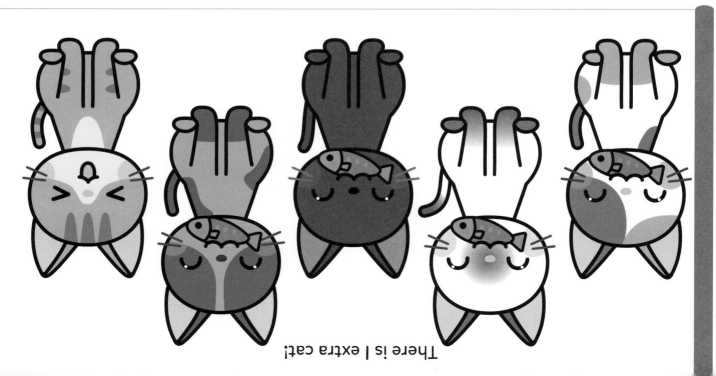

There is 1 extra cat!

Which Has the Most?

To Parents: Let your child guess which plate has the most candy on it without counting the chocolate bars. When done, ask your child which plate has the least.

Which plate has the most chocolate bars? Color the ◯ below the plate that has the most candy on it.

Which Is the Longest?

To Parents: In this activity, your child will practice comparing the lengths of different objects. Point out that the objects all start in the same place. You can also point out where each object ends to help your child compare them.

Which vehicle is the longest? Color the ◯ next to the longest vehicle.

Find the Matches

To Parents: Encourage your child to experiment with the hamburger cutouts. Can they put them in order from smallest to largest? How does each one fit in each box? Talk about small, medium, and large. Then, let them try pasting.

Sticker
Good job!

 Which box is the best size to hold each hamburger? Paste them in each box.

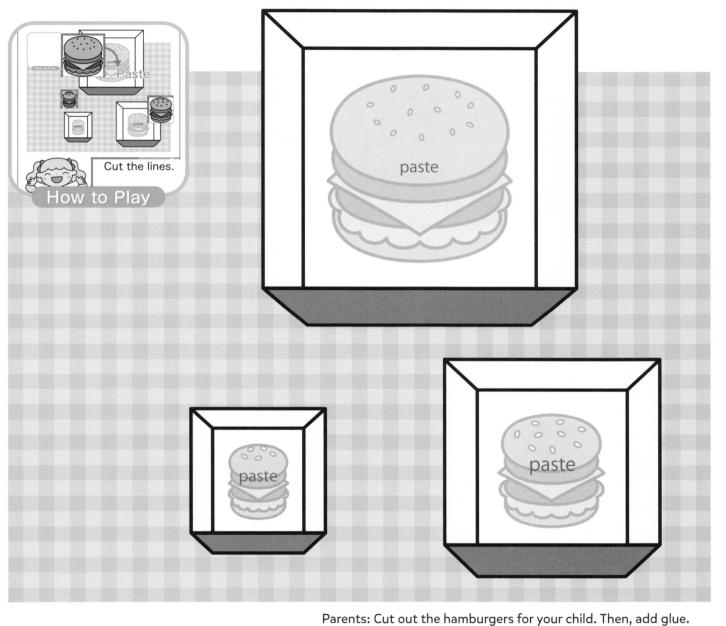

How to Play

Paste

Cut the lines.

paste

paste

paste

Parents: Cut out the hamburgers for your child. Then, add glue.

Which Is Longer?

To Parents: Ask your child to point to the longer truck. If they have difficulty, try comparing the number of wheels and storage trailers. You may also draw a line under each truck and compare lengths.

 Which truck is longer? Color the ⚪ next to the longer truck.

glue

glue

glue

Which Is the Longest?

To Parents: Have your child try to answer the question intuitively by simply looking at the wiggly snakes. Provide your child with safety scissors and encourage them to cut the page along the gray line.

  Which is the longest snake? Color the ◯ below the longest snake.
Cut along the gray line and fold along the dotted line to confirm your answer.

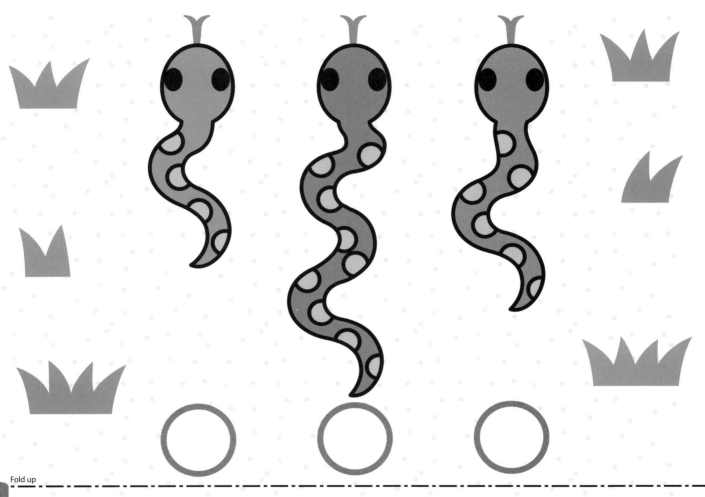

Fold up

How to Play

 Sticker

Good job!

Draw Using the Number 6

To Parents: Ask your child if they can see how the example drawing turned the number 6 into a bird. Then, ask them to draw to turn the 6 into something new.

 Count the flowers and trace the number 6 from ➡ to ➡. Then, draw to make something new out of the number 6.

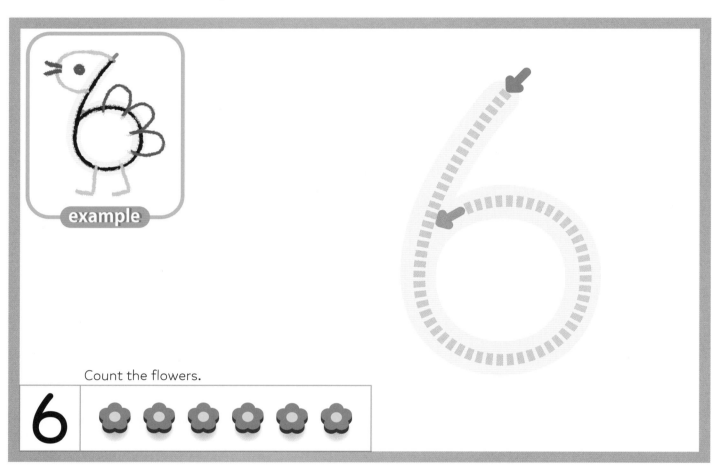

example

Count the flowers.

6 🌸 🌸 🌸 🌸 🌸 🌸

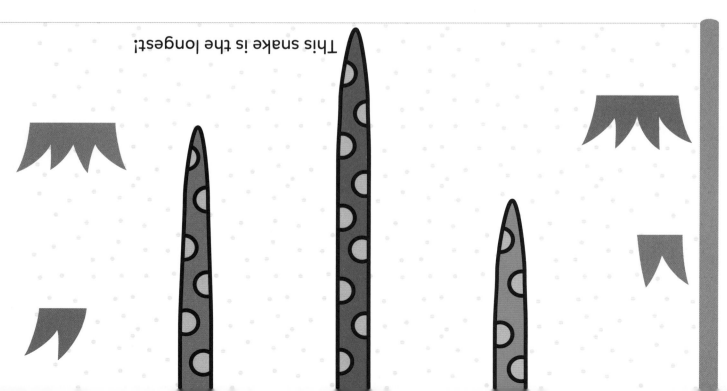

This snake is the longest!

Draw Using Your Hand Outline

To Parents: Ask your child to press their palm down on the page as you trace. Count the fingers aloud as you go. Show your child the example and encourage them to come up with a unique design.

  Count the flowers. Then, draw to make something new out of the shape of your hand!

example

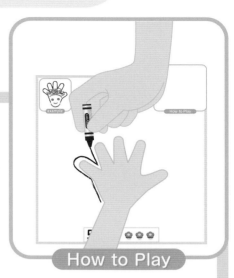
How to Play

Count the flowers.

5

Draw Using the Number 8

To Parents: Demonstrate tracing the number 8, starting with the pink arrow and ending with the blue arrow. Grab a blank piece of paper and demonstrate making the number 8 look like a person or a snowman. This is a great activity to enhance imagination.

  Count the flowers and trace the number 8 from ➡ to ➡. Then, draw outlines of ears, arms, and legs to finish the raccoon picture.

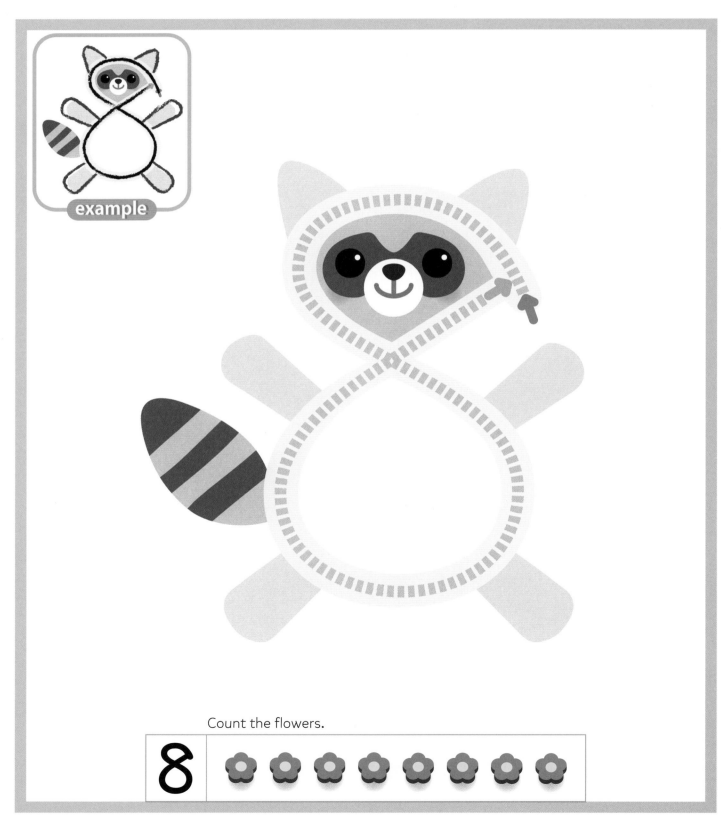

example

Count the flowers.

8 🌸🌸🌸🌸🌸🌸🌸🌸

Draw Using the Number 9

To Parents: Some children remember the shape of a number better when they visualize it as an object that's meaningful to them. Let your child try to come up with an object to enhance their imagination and creativity.

  Count the flowers and trace the number 9 from ➡ to ➡. Then, draw to turn it into something else.

example

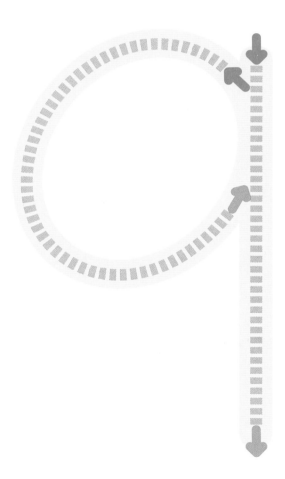

Count the flowers.

 q

Count the Vehicles

To Parents: Ask your child to point to and press on each vehicle as they count. Then, talk about the separate groups. When done, count all the vehicles.

 Count the ambulances. Then, write that number. Do the same for the buses.

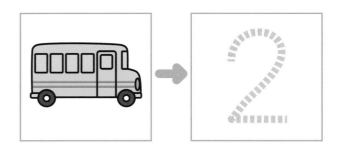

Count the Monsters

To Parents: Ask your child to start by counting the green monsters. Encourage them to point to and press on each monster as they count or they can circle each monster as they count each group.

 Count the green monsters. Then, write that number. Do the same for the other monsters.

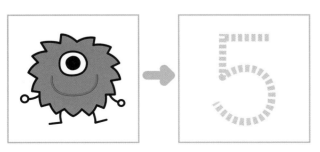

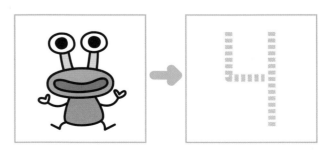

Count the Animals

To Parents: When there are no arrows to guide tracing, ask your child if they remember where to start and stop. If not, remind them.

Trace the number in the box. Then, color each animal. When you are finished coloring, count each group of animals aloud.

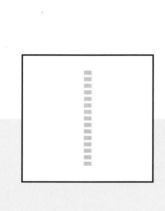

Count the Flowers

To Parents: Encourage your child to name each object and its quantity aloud (example: four sunflowers, five tulips). Your child can choose which they want to do first: coloring, tracing, or counting.

  Trace the numbers in the boxes. Color each flower. Count each group of flowers aloud.

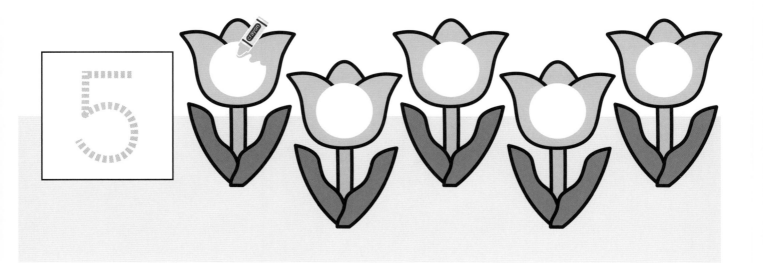

Count the Sweets

To Parents: Begin by providing safety scissors for your child to cut out the sweets. Encourage them to place each cutout with the group to which it belongs. Then, ask them to apply glue to the cutouts and paste them onto the page.

 Trace the numbers in the boxes. Cut out and paste the missing sweets. Then, count the total number of sweets in each group.

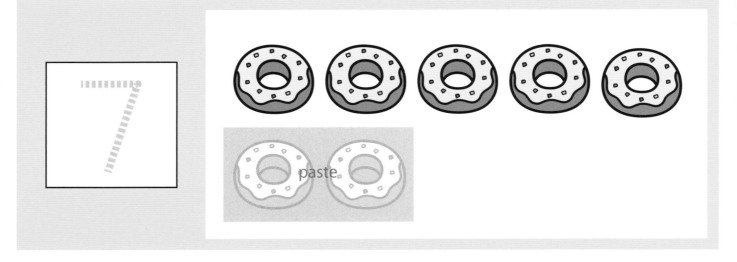

Count the Sweets

To Parents: Begin by providing safety scissors for your child to cut out the sweets. Encourage them to place each cutout with the group to which it belongs. Together, count to nine. Then, count to ten. When counting, pause after five, then continue.

  Trace the numbers in the boxes. Cut out and paste the missing sweets. Then, count the total number of sweets in each group.

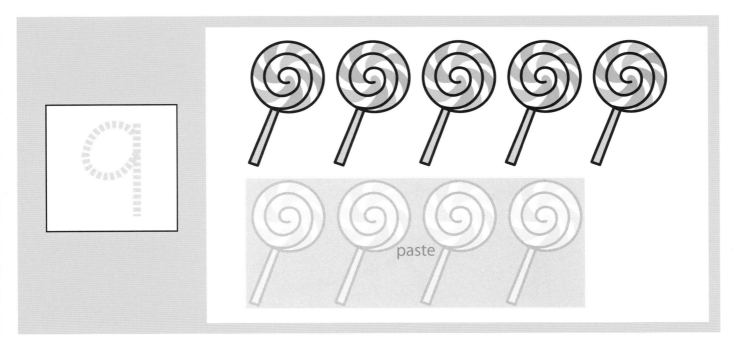

● For page 41

● For page 40 ● For page 40

Color by Number

To Parents: Begin by asking your child to find the number 2 in the picture. Outline the shape around the 2 in red. Then, ask your child to color that shape red. Do the same with brown each time your child finds the number 3.

Color the numbered shapes: 2 = red, 3 = brown. What do you see?

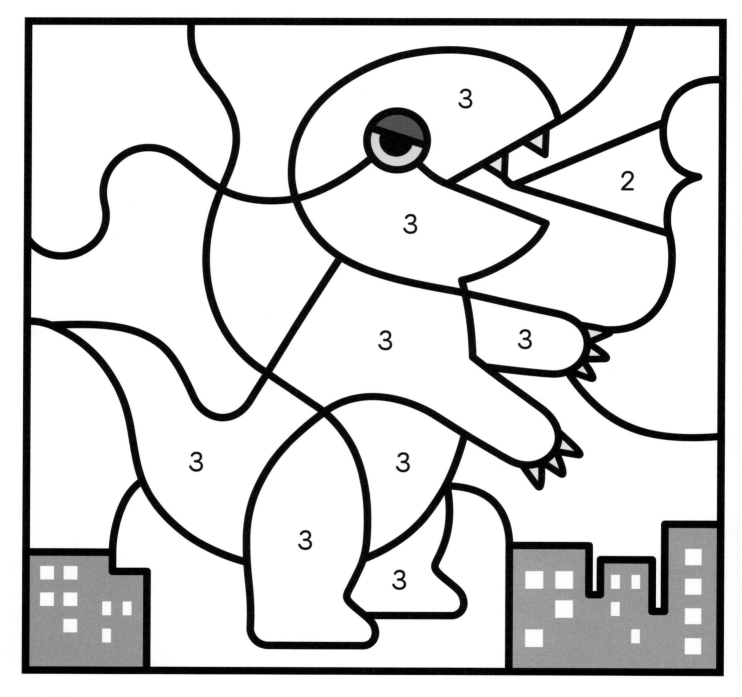

glue

glue

glue

Color by Number

To Parents: Begin by asking your child to find the number 9 in the picture. Outline the shape around the 9 in green yourself. Then, ask your child to color that shape green. Do the same with yellow and red each time your child finds the numbers 5 and 7.

 Color the numbered shapes: 5 = yellow, 7 = red, 9 = green. What do you see?

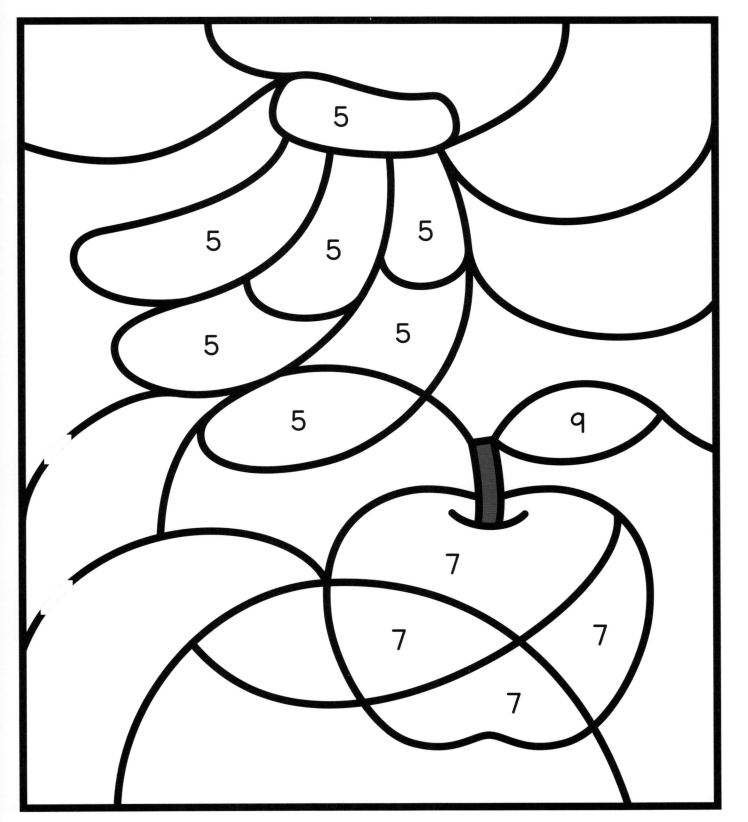

Fold to Make New Shapes

To Parents: Numbers are an important element in learning math, but shapes are just as important. It is critical for your child to learn shape recognition from an early age. Encourage your child to say "heart" and "circle" each time they put a sticker on the robot. Ask your child to name the shapes after they fold too.

Place the heart and circle stickers on the robot. Then, fold along the dotted lines for a surprise!

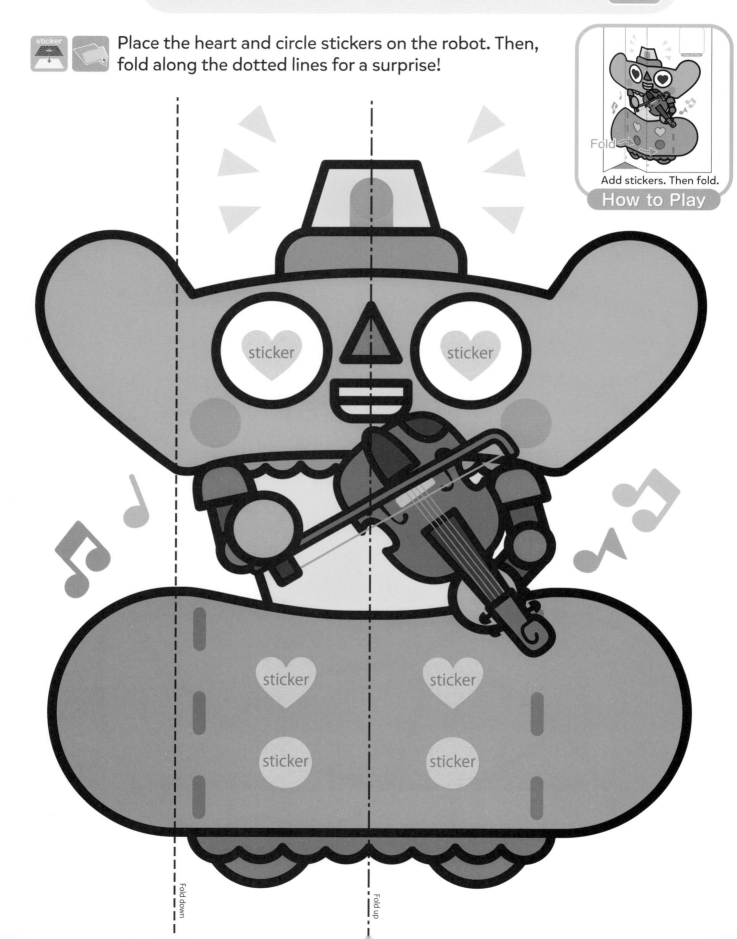

Fold

Add stickers. Then fold.

How to Play

sticker
sticker
sticker
sticker
sticker
sticker

Fold down

Fold up

Fold to Make New Shapes

To Parents: Numbers are an important element in learning math, but shapes are just as important. It is critical for your child to learn shape recognition from an early age. Can your child guess what shapes the robot will make when folded? Have them fold the page and say the names of the shapes they see.

Good job!

Sticker

 Fold along the dotted lines for a surprise!

How to Play

Fold

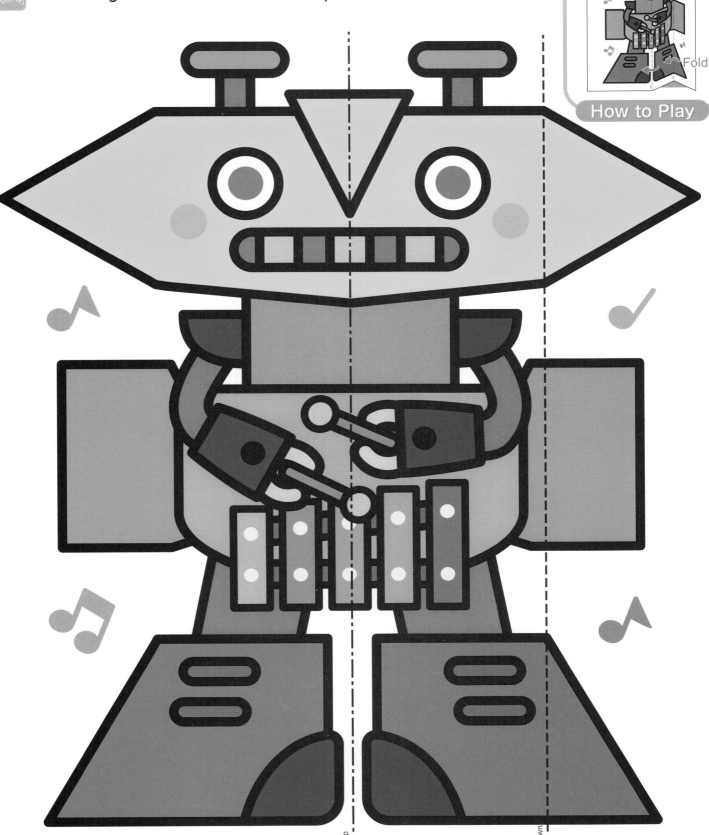

Fold up

Fold down

46

Search and Find Shapes

To Parents: Your child can practice their observation skills by looking for the shapes hidden in this picture. Search together for examples of different shapes in your home as well.

 Can you name the 4 shapes at the bottom of the page? Draw a line to connect each shape to the same shape in the picture.

example

SQUARE

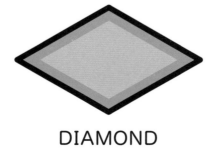
DIAMOND

HEART

CIRCLE

Search and Find Shapes

To Parents: Identifying an object's shape by its outline is a difficult activity for young children. Focus on one shape at a time. You may want to guide your child's finger to trace the object. Then, encourage them to trace each shape on the right until they find a match.

 Can you name the 5 shapes on the right of the page? Draw a line to connect each shape to the same shape in the picture.

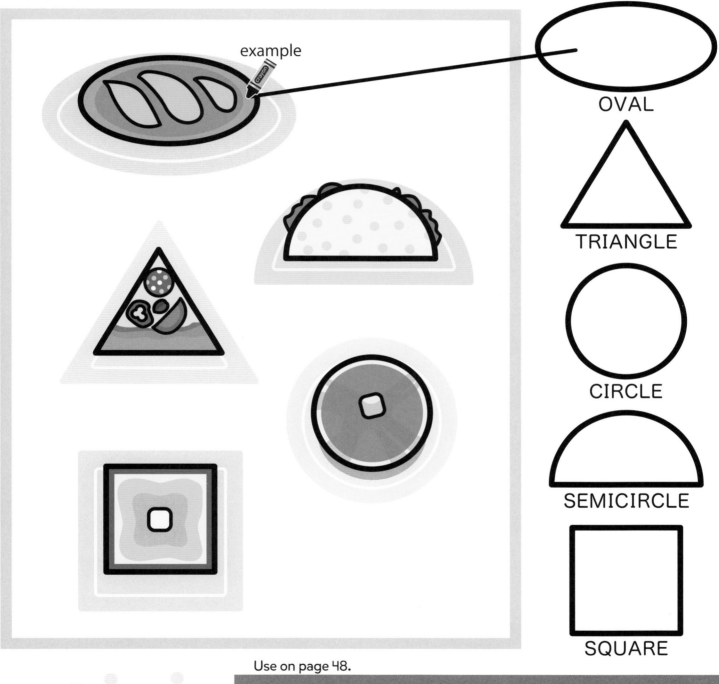

example

OVAL

TRIANGLE

CIRCLE

SEMICIRCLE

SQUARE

Use on page 48.

| glue | glue | glue | glue |

48

Good job!

Put Numbers in Order

To Parents: In this activity, your child will practice putting numbers in order. Help your child to cut out the numbers first. Ask them to count from 1 to 5. Then, see if they can put the number cutouts in order before they add glue.

Cut out and paste the numbers in order from smallest to biggest. Then, add the missing animals.

Put Numbers in Order

To Parents: Help your child cut out the numbers first. Count aloud from 1 to 10 together. Then, ask your child to put the circles in order before adding glue.

 Cut out and paste the numbers in order from smallest to biggest.

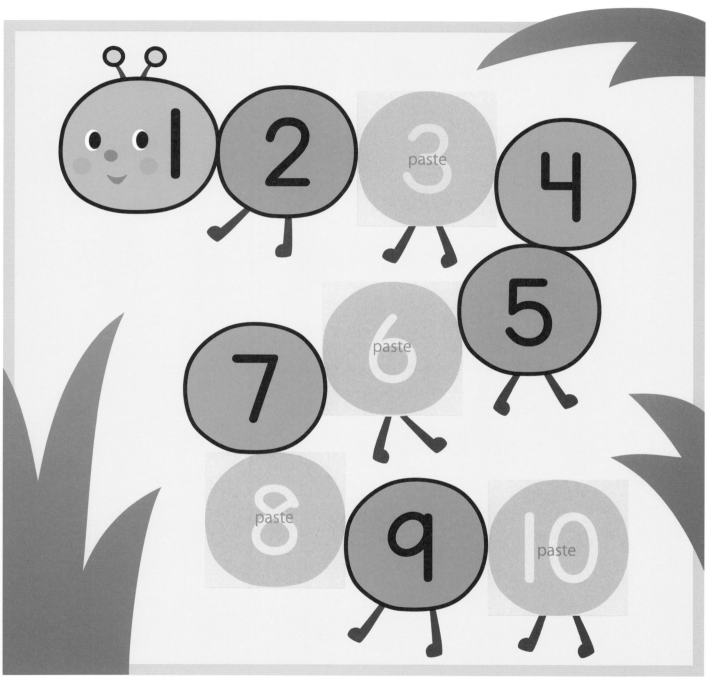

Connect the Dots

To Parents: Start by counting aloud from 1 to 5 with your child. Then, trace from dot to dot with a finger as you count. Ask your child to say the numbers aloud while connecting the dots. If needed, guide your child's hand when they try with a crayon.

 Draw a line from ● to ●. Start at 1 and end at 5.

glue	glue	glue	glue

Connect the Dots

To Parents: Start by counting aloud from 1 to 10 with your child. Then, trace from dot to dot with a finger as you count. Ask your child to say the numbers aloud while connecting the dots. If needed, guide your child's hand when they try with a crayon.

 Draw a line from ● to ●. Start at 1 and end at 10. Color the panda's eyes.

Use on page 52.

glue	glue	glue	glue	glue	glue

Make a Pattern

To Parents: Practicing pattern recognition is also an important foundational skill in math. After finishing this activity, try familiarizing your child with patterns by pointing out some examples around you (on clothing, toys, etc.) on a daily basis.

 Cut out the missing pieces and glue them to the page to complete the pattern: frog, ladybug, frog, ladybug.

● For page 52

● For page 53

Make a Pattern

To Parents: Practicing pattern recognition is also an important foundational skill in math. Encourage your child to point to and press on the objects in the pattern, saying "spider, ghost, spider, ghost" before gluing the pieces to the page.

 Cut out the missing pieces and glue them to the page to complete the pattern: spider, ghost, spider, ghost.

Sticker
Good job!

Count and Add

To Parents: This activity will help your child visualize adding. Once your child has cut and creased the lines below, ask them to fold and unfold the page, saying "one fish and one more fish makes two fish."

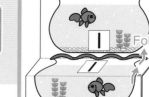
Fold
How to Play

There is 1 fish in the top bowl and 1 fish in the bottom bowl. How many total fish? Cut and fold the page and count to find out!

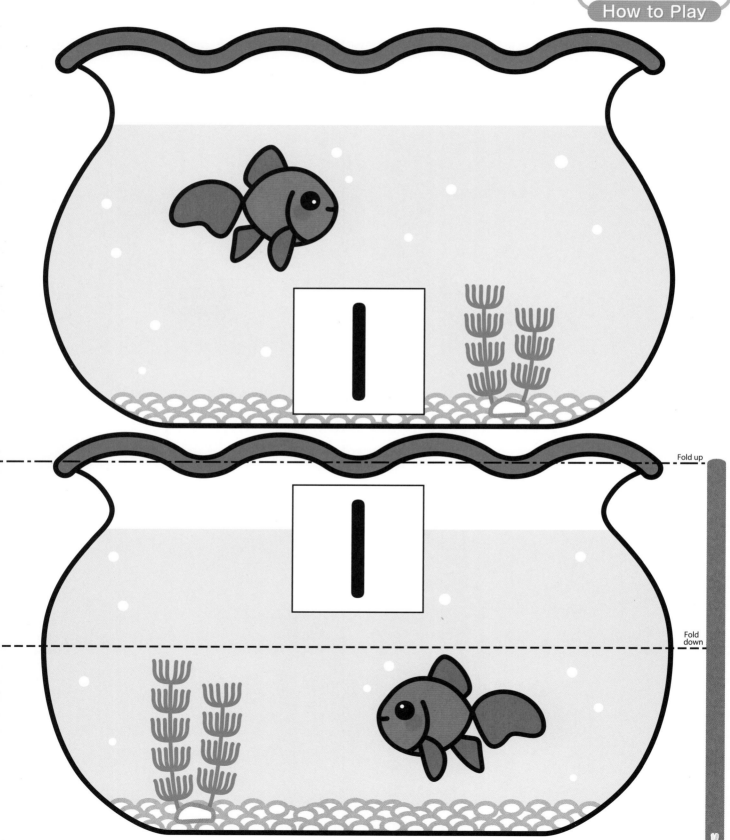

Fold up

Fold down

Count and Add

To Parents: Help your child to cut and crease the lines if they are having a hard time. Then, encourage them to fold and unfold the page, saying "two ducks and two more ducks makes four ducks." Repeat this many times to help your child understand the idea of addition naturally.

Sticker
Good job!

How to Play

There are 2 ducks in the top tub and 2 ducks in the bottom tub. How many total ducks? Cut and fold the page and count to find out!

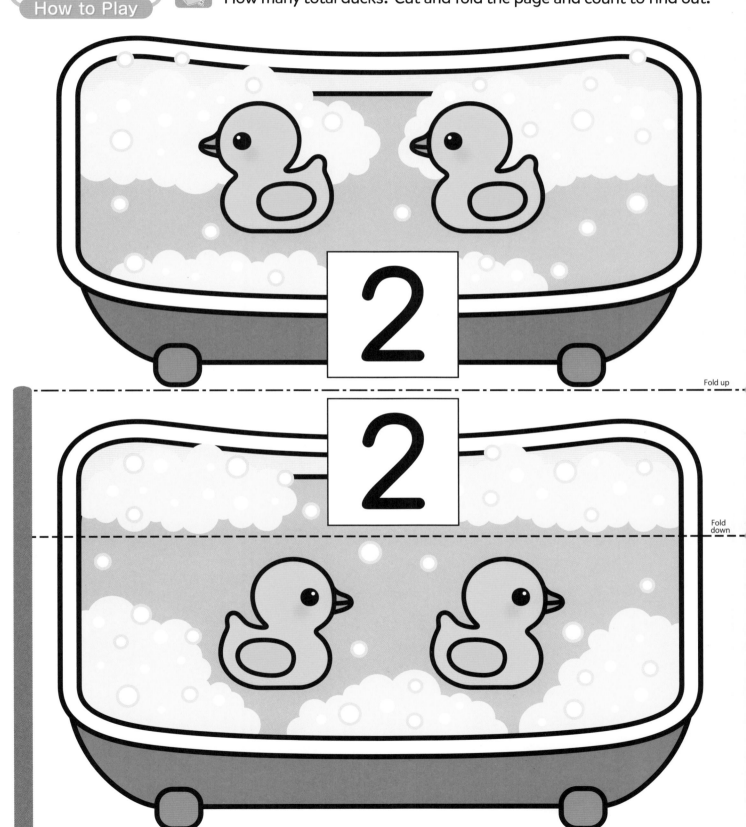

2

2

Fold up

Fold down

Count and Add

To Parents: Encourage your child to fold and unfold the page, saying "three cookies and two more cookies makes five cookies." Try adding with objects around you, such as blocks.

How to Play

There are 3 cookies in the top bag and 2 cookies in the bottom bag. How many total cookies? Cut and fold the page and count to find out!

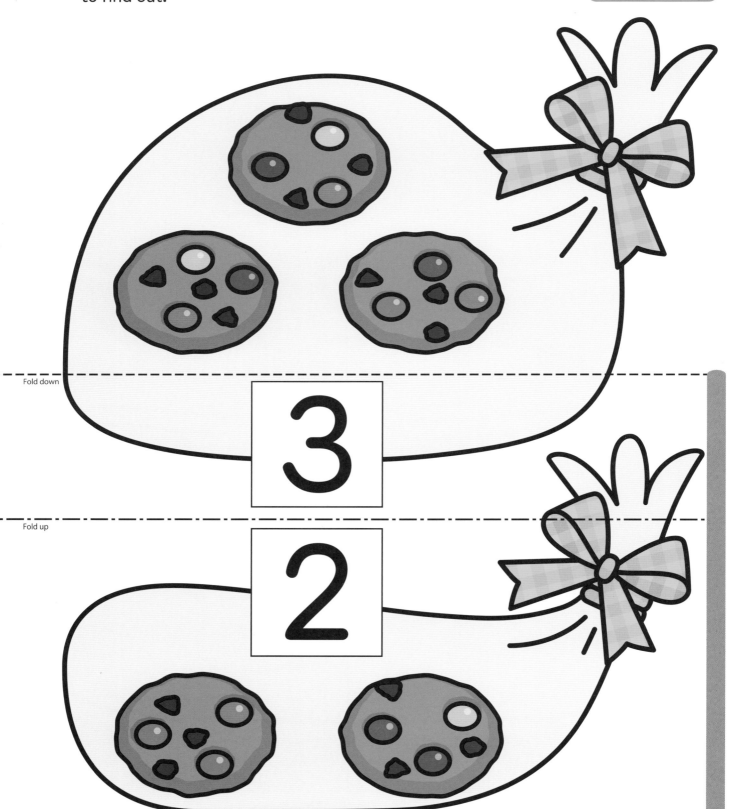

Fold down

Fold up

Count and Add

How to Play

To Parents: In addition to folding and unfolding the page while saying "three cupcakes and three more cupcakes makes six cupcakes," ask your child to point to and press on each cupcake as they count the total.

Sticker

Good job!

There are 3 cupcakes in the top box and 3 cupcakes in the bottom box. How many total cupcakes? Cut and fold the page and count to find out!

3

Fold up

3

Fold down

Connect the Dots

To Parents: Before starting this activity, visit page 1 and 60 and count aloud from 1 to 15 with your child. If necessary, trace from dot to dot with a finger and count aloud before providing a crayon.

Draw a line from ● to ●. Start at 1 and end at 15.

Connect the Dots

To Parents: Before starting this activity, visit page 1 and 60 and count aloud from 1 to 20 with your child. If necessary, trace from dot to dot with a finger and count aloud before providing a crayon.

Draw a line from ● to ●. Start at 1 and end at 20.

Counting 11 to 20

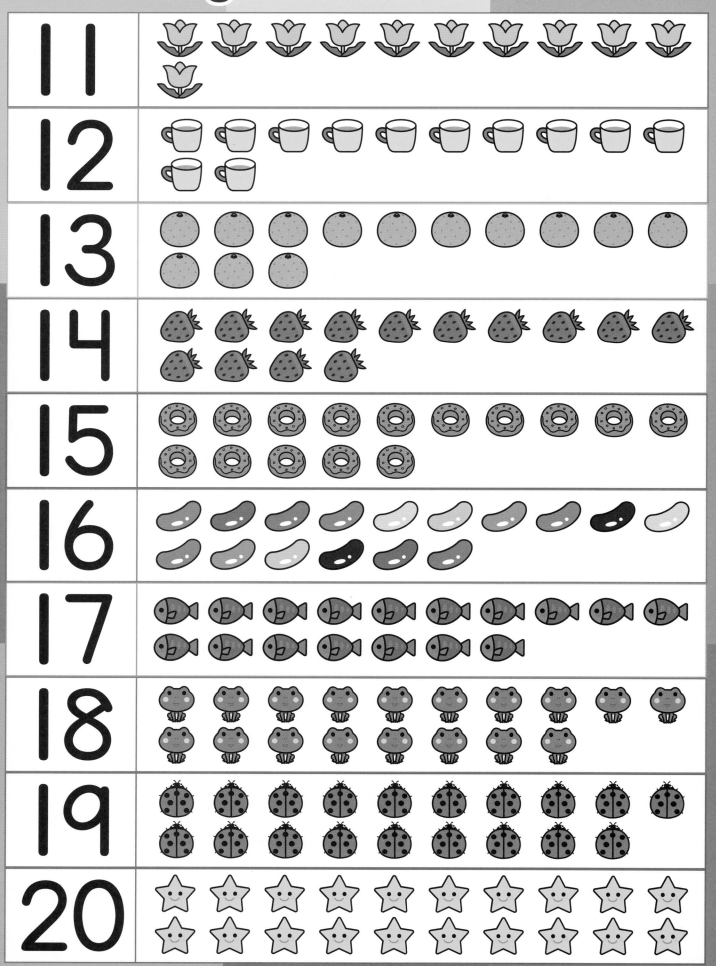

Foldout PICTURE BOOK

• How to Play •

★ Count from 1 to 12. Use the numbers on the paper as your guide.

7 hamburgers!

★ Hang the paper on the wall like a garland.

1 2 3 4 5!

★ Fold the paper to make a book.

Where is 7?

Here!

★ Lay the paper flat. Say a number out loud. Ask your child to point to the number you say. Flip over the paper and keep playing.

Fold down

Fold up

Fold down

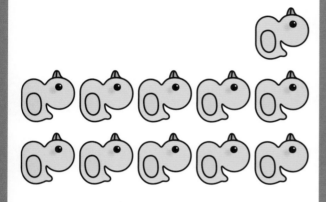

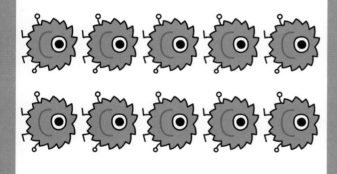

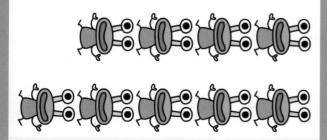

1 Cut along the gray lines.

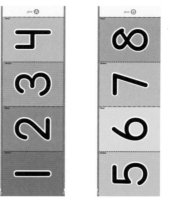

2 Paste glue **A** to paste **A**,
glue **B** to paste **B**

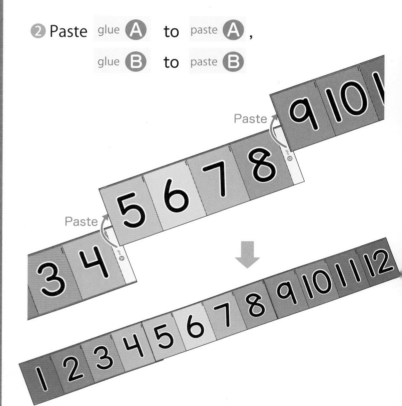

Paste
Paste

3 Fold along the dotted lines.

— — — Fold down   — · — · Fold up

Finished

Fold up

Fold up

Fold down

Fold down

Fold up

Fold up

Fold down

Fold down

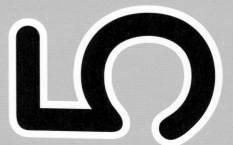

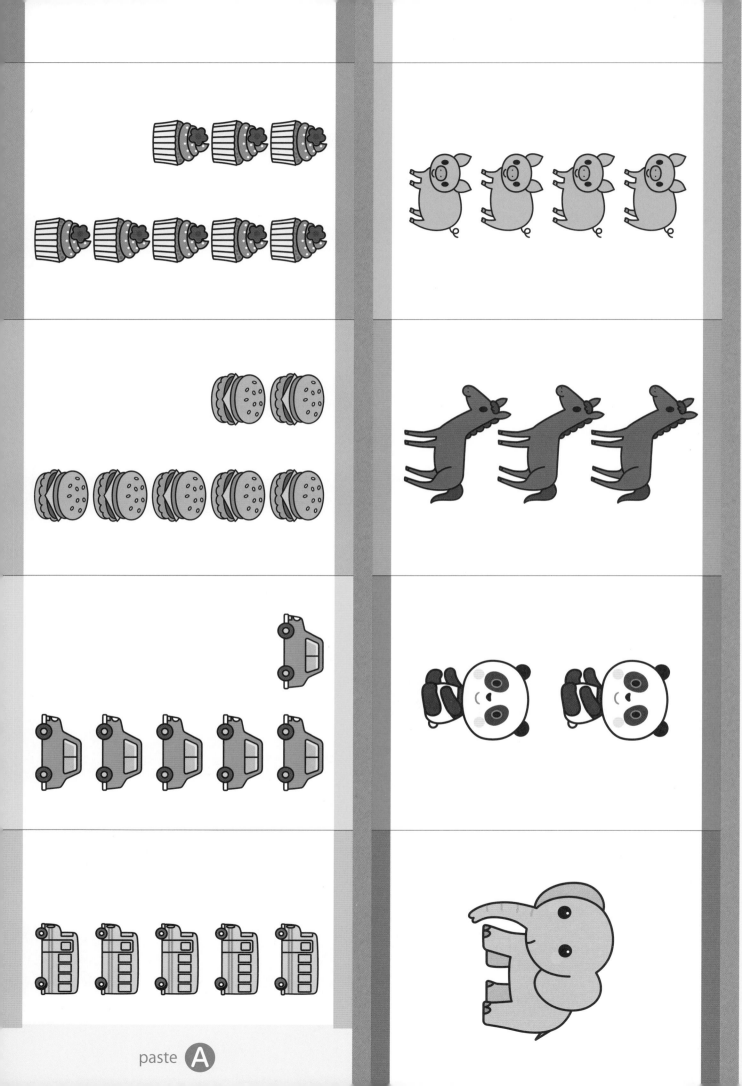

WIPE-CLEAN Numbers Board

Let's write the numbers by tracing the lines.

1

2

3

4

5

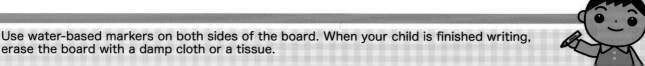

Let's write the numbers by tracing the lines.

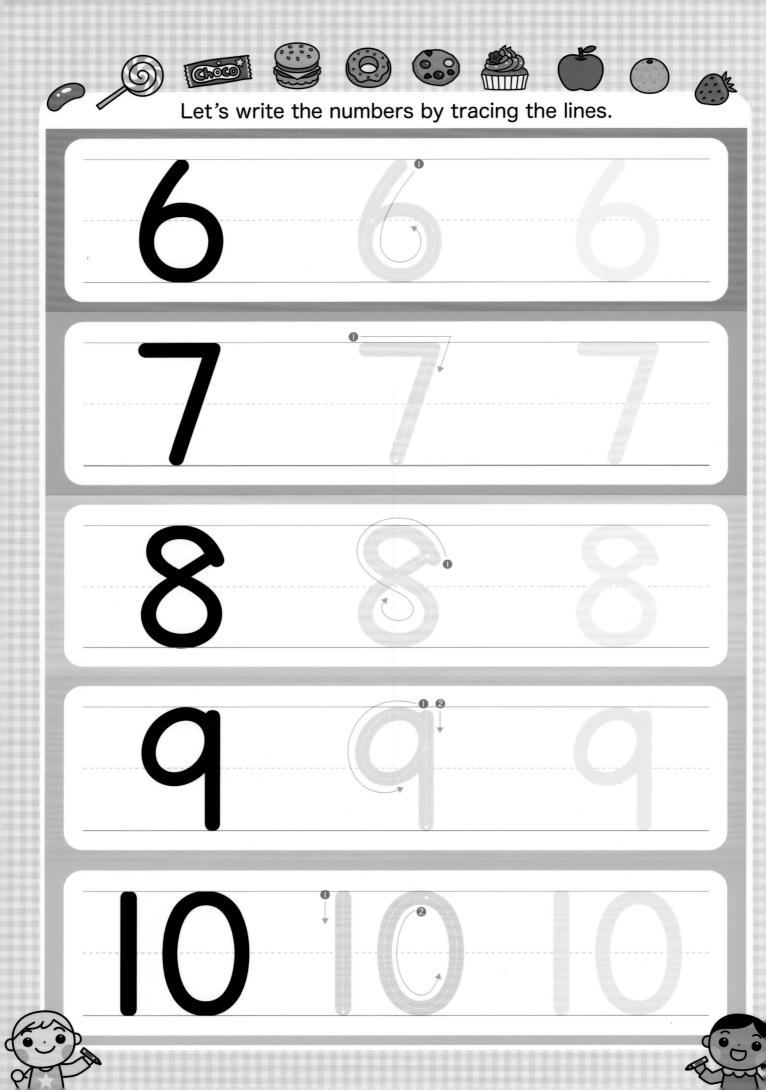